OR WHAT
WE'LL CALL
DESIRE

ALSO BY ALEXANDRA TEAGUE

POETRY

Bullets into Bells: Poets & Citizens Respond to Gun Violence
(as co-editor)

The Wise and Foolish Builders

Mortal Geography

FICTION

The Principles Behind Flotation: A Novel

OR WHAT WE'LL CALL DESIRE

POEMS

ALEXANDRA TEAGUE

A KAREN & MICHAEL BRAZILLER BOOK
PERSEA BOOKS / NEW YORK

Request for permission or for information should be addressed to the publisher:

Persea Books, Inc.
90 Broad Street
New York, NY 10004

Library of Congress Cataloging-in-Publication Data

Names: Teague, Alexandra, 1974– author.
Title: Or what we'll call desire : poems / Alexandra Teague.
Other titles: Or what we will call desire
Description: First edition. | New York : Persea Books, [2019] | "A Karen & Michael Braziller Book."
Identifiers: LCCN 2019012339 | ISBN 9780892554997 (original trade paperback : alk. paper)
Classification: LCC PS3620.E42 A6 2019 | DDC 811/.6—dc23
LC record available at https://lccn.loc.gov/2019012339

Book design and composition by Rita Lascaro
Typeset in Mendoza
Manufactured in the United States of America. Printed on acid-free paper.

CONTENTS

OR WHAT
WE'LL CALL
DESIRE

Self Portrait as *Curious Lunatic's Sketch of a Dancing Girl*

An odd conception is the extra pair of eyes in the woman's hat.
The American Weekly, *1921*

I'll tell it again: after my mother died, I danced on her chairs
in mad circles. It was only dancing because there was music
in another room. I needed her kitchen to be a carousel:
not flour, tablespoons, hands—but bright lacquered stallions

and bridles. I was only living because someone was breathing
inside my lungs. I needed extra eyes just to see her—her
hands as tablespoons of ash. I lacquered myself with bright
broken mirrors. I wanted the woman at Civic Center station

to be the tree she said she was. I needed more eyes to look
away. When men held her back, she cried, *Don't cut my branches.*
We needed that train to hit us so we had reason to be broken.
It wasn't just my mother. I was always afraid. I gave men

the saw and then cried, *Don't cut my branches.* Cried, *hold me
together* as I made self a collage. I feared both too much and
too little. It wasn't just my mother, therapied back into 1962,
out of phase with self once, too, like a horror movie voice.

I was always collaging fear with cheaply built carnivals.
I climbed on the stallion, the ostrich, the fun house mirror.
Out of phase as the voice in *The Exorcist*—that corner of
mechanical and human, I curled up drunk in a police car

between the ostrich-feather palm trees of Key West. I
climbed in by choice. At the corner of Mechanical and
Human, I kept drunkenly asking the police to call
the number of the phone I was carrying. Who was I ever

but a girl climbing through the choices of being human?
Who was I as I slipped pills inside to slip outside myself
to dance? Some nights, I was the right number on redial.
When my nephew went mad, I said, *if our mother weren't dead,*

this would kill her. He swallowed pills to slip outside the self
who read Flannery O'Connor aloud in the cemetery to honor
her birthday. If she weren't dead, he would have let her pet
his pet rabbit. When he went mad, he spoke like a Western-

movie version of himself—born to gravel and the loud
grit of necessity. Anne Carson writes this is where the soul
is. I was there when we buried him in a Western cemetery.
I helped carry his body. It was his 26th birthday. Did he

need that gun to explain why he was broken? What do any of us
become when we subtract the world, or add its necessities
to the grit and the lacquer? I will never not carry his body.
I will never not dance with these extra eyes in my hat.

In the Case of Mlle. Zina Brozia of the Paris Grand Opera Versus M. Jean Metzinger, Cubist

1916

A woman posing for a portrait expects

        her face, not a radio sputtering

disassembled circuits, a madman tatting

        her collar like a hedge on the asylum lawn

loop after loop of lace and so many throats

        the notes would never find their way

it's dangerous

        calling this a body, art, what aria

ever sang out of the ear of the beloved

        triangle line line circle

what portrait painter worth his easel

        could believe as this one claims

this is the sum of what will be remembered

        when she passes out of vision's range

as if the sum of 1 plus 3 were muskrat

        just subtract a plum, then add a dirigible,

a spoon, Your Honor, this is not

        as you say, *a delicate controversy,*

not that model who sued over Aphrodite's

        shell: in question, should she have to supply it

was it essential to the pose like Eve's leaf

I understand delicacy: woman naked on nothing

in the painted ocean but I am not a ship

radioing SOS, dits and dahs all run together, an abacus

in a windstorm   what Salome

no matter how wild with love, desperate-

cursing at her mother, could lift her hand to die

if she couldn't first distinguish

the dagger's fatal line from her own body?

The Giant Artichoke

I'm so many people. Sometimes, I wish I was just me.
Marilyn Monroe

I am a child posing beneath thirty feet of leaves
that bloom and bristle like the sound of fighter jets
drilling above desert highways where my mother reads
each peeling billboard because without words what are we

but ourselves—inarticulate as the sky, as the fighter jets
to explain their sound; as my mother's father to explain
how it felt to drown, though she listened, peeling back
the ocean leaf by leaf. I am beneath the fanned, hooked

shelter of those leaves. Matryoshkaed inside my mother's
grief: our clawfoot bathtub drain repeating how a ship
can sink and sink and sink. His dying fanned like leaves
nesting the choke nesting the grey-green heart I learned

to find. Heaps of clawed debris repeating how hunger
peels back, and underneath: hunger's more pointed leaves.
I learned love as rituals of hunger, a nest of thistles
around the heart. At best, temporary gleams of butter.

I stand as my mother's camera peels back to fields
then zooms to me in this promised land—the sunlight
lemoning massive plaster leaves. Permanent, gleaming
as if they'll fill our hungers with what we cannot eat.

My grandmother, who lived to eighty in the desert sun,
wrote in her journal once that none of it seemed real.
Nothing she ate. Nothing she saw. Not even her hunger.
The real ended at a railing in World War II, the sea

bright as butter on a child's mouth, unwriteably blue
as the satin sash of a beauty queen. Here in Castroville,
Marilyn (barely not Norma Jean) was crowned in a sea
of thistles, first Artichoke Festival Queen. Starlet pinned

to herself, the long spaces between. Here in Castroville,
I am in artichoke heaven; we've come from the desert,
my grandmother's house, where, pinned between waking
and dream, I've seen a saguaro stand by the couch—

raising heaven-strange arms like a man on a ship.
Her lost father followed Marilyn too, slipped inside her
dreamy smile; her hands raising artichokes, in one ad,
like green grenades. Still as a cast of myself at dawn,

I saw the recliner—raised, its arms—but could not follow
logic to believe the world was ever one thing. I'd seen
walls peel back. I stood beside head-high leaves, child
posed at the center of this picture that is not of me.

End Times

It's why God invented abstract art:
so we'd have a way of imagining—
that torn-open pink that's stormcloud and caution line and nowhere
we've been yet. Japanese brushstrokes
meet Hiroshima meet Pandora's
Black Friday salesbox, all its curling
ribbon, pretty wrapping. We opened it. We knelt there laughing at the _____.
I was joking about God. I'm serious
about how it feels to watch the world
unravel. At the science museum, walls
of glaciers photographed before & after. Like perfect weight-loss ads. It's
irreversible. This going-on-living. *Rain*
again in Texas; my ex-husband texting
each day's weather, new paintings. Crosses these days instead of splashes.
This is all foretold, he texts, *in Revelation. U can*
read it. He knows the statistics on suicide
among the bipolar; he's winning. God
may be his new abstraction. Triangles may be beams from heaven. *Sunny. Strangely*
warm for Nov. I've quit saying *Climate change*
because he'll just bring up horsemen. So
much art is titled *Untitled* for good reason.
Temperatures mean *Hello, I'm alive.* Like it's neutral.
I'm the one with a car, too much flying. *It's cloudy* today. There are squiggles
like confetti at New Year's, fear sparkled up
under laughter, fraying ropes, an exploded sun. *What do u think?* he texts. Before
Nowhere near done.

Baba Yaga Rides It's a Small World

Dear dolls: do not believe Freud that your almost
aliveness is what frightens: that you *are* yet *are not*.
No one believes Dutch girls wear folded paper hats
and carry tulips. Except Donald Trump. Except anger
and men who make islands. Tell them
about islands. Tell them about glue: how the sweet parade
wave you have perfected is gesture as lacquer,
elbow-elbow, wrist-wrist. It's not a talent to throw tulips
that never leave your hands. You know the windmill
like it is your dirty-fingered brother; like it is the red pagoda
plus arms, one singing room away. It's all the same sea,
dyed with copper sulfate until the blue is uncanny.
Like womb water. Like the sea of repression.
That doesn't mean these people fear castration
at your tiny hands; that you might pluck their eyes
from their heads. They'd give those freely
for Mouse Ears. For a wood-fingered double
who knows how to scrub dishes—how,
in some fairytales, to trick witches. Dear dolls,
have you noticed no one steps onto your shores?
That's because it's illegal. No one knows
your stiff-legged patriotic dance. Tell us what you've
done with all the guns. It's a small world for airplanes
and Ebola, for a girl facedown on classroom tiles
pretending dead when the shooter says
"raise your head." Dear people, are you frightened yet?
Freud was right about compulsion. You have sex dolls
to prove it. You have maquiladoras where women paint
smiles. You have primitive urges. You've heard it
deep inside your psyche: *Climb out of the boat*
of reason. What can you do about this world
but wave and wave and wave and wave and wave?

Driving After Rain

The self like silverware laid out finally for a feast. Bright
lanes of light along the gorge this morning, that watery rush

like the waterwheel I used to love to go see at the mill:
the War Eagle gushing brown Southern babble

over sunspots of stone, dark flecks of childhood
lifted into swinging buckets, rain pockmarks of *failure*

or *giver* or *grief* churning not in transubstantiation but in water
rising up as water, holy in the hands of old oak;

Oh God, make them like a wheel, not a curse, but a way
to ride the whole way around our bodies

and back—like once in the front seat by an L.A. highway,
I'd pull over with a man, a storm

so blinding rain blinding no one saw my skirt lifting
against steering wheel; we were always driving nowhere

and it didn't matter then, suspended
like water I don't quite understand, how it falls fast enough

to carry itself up and over and still be whole
the way I pretended I wasn't—knowing he was lying

that he'd ever love me, throwing myself anyway
like this river was everything. *As stubble before the wind.*

Inside that mill, flour dusts every skin. So what
if I'm dammed and damned and driven; some days

I'm also shining like spoons milled by water, bread
my mother kneaded as I set knife beside fork—hunger

taught to be orderly as wheels at fairs, that sky-swinging danger
with its sturdy spokes like psalms splitting the word of God

from the water of every other word.

Requiem for No Hands

Because she was angry; did not have a piano
in their small, North Side apartment; did not know the music
to the first big fight after the wedding dress
was bagged in plastic like a body, its infinite beads
unprismed on a shelf. Because of the plywood-
and-carpet silence the door left as it swung closed

behind her husband, the way it stayed closed
in false expectation, like my mother's piano-
teacher eyes on her hands: the keys' wood
waiting for more thunderous, perfect music
than she could ever play. All those dark beads
strung across the staff of one great Baroque dress

she could not unravel, like her wedding-dress
vow of love, the hope chest she'd closed
with God as her witness—the hard abacus beads
tallying up to forever. She had no piano
to practice; no other life to learn the music
she'd been given. Maybe she hoped she would

scare him; maybe she imagined he would
save her: passed out in the kitchen, her dress
soft as gas fumes—her body distant as chamber music
from some far-off concert. Maybe she closed
the windows, imagining applause—a piano
she alone could play—the light in sharp beads

across its Black Sea gleam, the air beaded
with anticipation as she found each note the wood
held in it. Maybe she never thought of pianos
as she turned the gas on. Maybe she told her dress
goodbye in the closet, prayed, bolted the still-closed
door so her husband would find her music

already played. I remember little of the music
my mother taught, patient as rosary beads,
at that piano. Not that woman's name, closed
in some lost book of concertos. Only the wooden
bench where she didn't sit practicing, dressed
in young, grown-up laughter; the spinet piano

she was saving to buy after her wedding dress.
My mother playing—sweat-beaded, crying—music
she'd never teach; how the piano folded closed.

Ofelia Plays Like a Girl

Because no one tells her not to—not
at first: her hands like high-desert clouds,

more shadow than rain—she presses the piano's
pedal to sustain herself inside her skin: flicker

of tomboy on a barbed-wire fence—
pockets stuffed with bread for invisible

horses. Their hooves' soft notes. Dust storms
swirling between the bars of music. *Every good*

bird does. Fly-spangled buzz of afternoon.
Empty washes between keys. Her mother

in the kitchen—how the mixer sings
like Mozart's starling (she's read somewhere

he heard it in a pet store cage, whistling
his piano concerto in G in perfect time).

All cows eat grass. All music is caged inside
some body, some motor—some dry wind

rattling the metal on the porch. What more
can she be? Two hands scattering seeds.

Chord of sunburned and lonely and learning.
Girl with scorpions in the piano's strings.

Baba Yaga Appears in Intro to Feminist Theory for an Impromptu Lecture

"And has Baba Yaga really got iron teeth?" asked Vanya.
"Iron, like the poker and tongs," said old Peter.
"What for?" said Maroosia.
Old Peter's Russian Tales

Dear class: dear guy who just raised his hand again
to say the patriarchs were right
to be worried: women today are getting divorced-pregnant-
teenage-independent—just look at this country. Women are rising up
like winter under asphalt, crumbling this nation's highways
til the rumble strips make the sound of fraying nerves;
until the baby teeth inside the mouths of families jostle loose
and spit out bullets. (Yes, I know bullets aren't iron.)
Yes, I have seen the blood. It's like the Bible—
that part where God says *drive only in your lane or else the pig gets slaughtered*
(and also your daughter). That myth
where the woman is a cave,
a river no one can locate inside her. She moves room to room
to room: in each that noise like bristles of a giant broom
sweeping each trace of her passing.
Let's call the broom
patriarchy. Let's call the girl *Zelda.* Let's say she holds
her father's hand like a lion tamer holds the hoop, hoping
danger sees its shiny ring and plunges through it.
Let's say she has no father. Her father beats her.
The cave of her body is overflowing with blind,
electric fish. She has surgery to remove the river, but
when the surgeon looks inside, he finds a pair of
ancient silver scissors. They've already cut
through her. Remember how a woman
is always divided? Who left those scissors inside her?
Once upon a time, last year, a woman
was hog-tied in a neighborhood park, stabbed until she died
a mile from here. Once upon a . . . A boy raised

his hand to say *You're confusing the system*
designed to protect you with anomalous violence. Dear boy,
you are making my teeth ache
like metal filings stuck in those patterns
on a guidance counselor's desk. Once upon, a girl
cried rape; cried beating; incest; silence; cried bullet; cried baby;
cried. You get the picture. (Or don't you?)
Do you know the difference between a woman wrapped in plastic
and a Christmas tree? A hula hoop and a hierarchy
built like a ladder with rungs to where a mother
is digging bomb rubble for the arm of her child?
Yes, hand-broom? *How ironic: we both agree women*
have natural maternal urges. Yes, I call myself
a witch. (See *witch* as anomaly.) (See *anomaly*: from *deviation*
from the common rule. From *inequality.*) Once upon a time,
we told a story so many times it ceased to be anomalous;
it remained anomalous. A girl drowned in the world's
river. A witch tried to point out the water. A hand-broom cried—
(see *cry:* from *squeal like a pig.*) (See witch. See Circe.)—
But you also eat children! (See Leviticus and Jeremiah.)
See the way my mouth moves. That terrible clacking.
That's statistics. 0% of the people in this room were not born
from a woman. 0% of your fairytales were written by fairies.
Yes, I agree we can learn valuable lessons. If you put your fingers inside
the rings on the handle and point the sharp tip up,
you can blind yourself with scissors.

The Hungry Eye

where I watch the stripper, who is stronger and more metallic
than the brass pole, hold herself upside down
like she's taken the whole carousel on its spindly
stick—horse horse ostrich boring sleigh—and flipped
it, and if there's any tinny music it's
her sternum making itself known to her heart;
it's her calf muscles making themselves
Vaselined art that could kick us skyward,
which is to say not art at all, not the catapult
Michael Stipe murmured from the dark kudzu of cassette—
mouthfuls of Southern rivers' silty pebbles
on his tongue (and did he like men or women
women or men we wanted to know as teenagers, wanting
his wanting to explain our own)—not an object but vibrations
of the stone mid-air before the river: brightness of
splash of brightness of water until we hardly saw
the shores inside us; the brass-sky-gleamed Mississippi
drowning farms along the highways one spring, all the signage floating,
and us, or was it only me, only
pretending surprise, as if I hadn't always felt
some state of high emergency inside me, some fear
of overflowing self in all directions: horses floating past fences
swollen and swallowed, clouds mixing with stop signs
like the blood-specked bathmat of my friend's boyfriend
on heroin again; she refused to see
pinpricks of blood outside the shower, needing
to believe his promise was a levee; his body
more than the pole desire was caught on
like we're all cotton candy at the county fair
of childhood: fill in the county name and let the dirty fluff
accumulate til we can't tell the sugar-light
from the choking—
Did we miss anything? Did we miss anything?—
howl of rope, of the question
and its answers catapulting toward us:

that girl who rode the J-Church
all one fall, each morning, cuticles jagged as notebook paper,
telling me—almost-stranger—about the women's
whips and ropes she chose, blue bruises like butterflies
fluttering her wrists, and me hearing *vanilla*
(my favorite flavor as a child) for the first time dulled
by its sweetness, like candles in Pottery Barn
we rode past in the Castro where I wanted not lampshades
not baskets but her body there, newly marked
in the day's afterimage of night's desires (the train's bright
jail-cell confessional) and only nodding
because after all, wasn't it only the idea of wanting?—
to know my edges; the rock of my body
caught mid air like light swinging off the rails at our eyes
like this woman's hair as she twists her thighs, clasping
hand-over-hand-over, body
swimming the river of desire, or what we'll call desire—
head under (only air and yet—) (how does anyone
know when is enough?) only long enough for pleasure.

Ode to Theda

America was on the cusp of something resembling sexual change,
but it wasn't quite there. It needed a half-naked vampire
with kohl-caked eyes to push [it] towards desire.
"Scandals of Classic Hollywood: The Most Wicked Face of Theda Bara"

Because who doesn't sometimes eat bones
in a dollhouse: pink Rose of Sharon on the wallpaper;

tea kettle shrieking like a cozy bat. Your bite:
what every man wanted as the hidden reason

for his collar, pressed and upright. A sexy sweep-
across-the-drum-skin brush with death. Your name

stretching mirror-writing shadows of pyramids
through Cincinnati's suburb streets. Terrorism,

even television, not quite there yet. Just the ordinary
terror of opposable thumbs. So much animal

beyond them. Why not zoo it up for the cameras?
Remind this country that domestication and satiation

just share a suffix: no nearer than china plates
and South China tigers. Lick the blood up

like the ketchup it is. They're wild about the wild
you. Who doesn't wish sometimes the stiff beautician

were the Sphinx come back with riddles of rollers
and small talk? What's half sweet-bred girl and all

vampire? Why did George Martinez push his wife
out the window? Testify for us (says the California court):

can't a vamp not be satisfied? Won't she spit men out
like teeth in a prizefight? What choice does a tired

husband have but self-preservation? Lie to us.
Say somewhere there's an apartment so full of sex sex

sex the windows shatter of their own accord. The vases
are desperate for water. Your eyes like blackout curtains

for air raids that aren't quite here yet. Like telescopes
scanning darkness for desire. Promise us nothing but this.

The Altogether

Audrey Munson, age 15, meets Isidore Konti, 1906

He told me I'd have to pose *in the altogether—*
He said it made no difference: clothing, fur,
or the body undraped of everything but its *entire*

form. True artists see only the work that we are
doing. And my mother set her teacup in its saucer:
such a faint white chiming of the wind and never.

And I heard what I didn't say. His statues bolder
than real women. The marble I could be, daughter
of a chisel. Molten bronze. I felt him look me over:

see what I already was—different, altogether,
than I'd known. Someone with rooftops inside her.
Someone gleaming and solid. The perfect center

of a set of Russian dolls. Bright baby. Bathwater
shimmer of self I'd throw anything off to uncover.

The Louvre Saloon, San Jose: Hatchetation, 1903

Truly does a saloon make a woman bare of all things.
Carry A. Nation

Somewhere inside, we are all cheap painted
velvet: sprawled nude with a choker of diamonds;
Jane Stanford's jewels—meticulous, accurate—oiled with spite
(by an artist she'd insulted) on a hooker and nailed in the Louvre saloon
so any drunkard could leer the pearled globes

of her pendants. Those light-drizzled lobes like Vermeer
mixed with "Like a Virgin" years before it played in a Texas pizzeria
and I first wondered—pepper flakes flaring my raw child tongue—
what it meant: something like souvenir fans unfolding firmaments of blooms
from their tight-clasped spines, like oil-tanker waves on the Gulf's

brown water; iridescent tapes unspooled in the highway grass;
men muscling crates of light onto the docks. Ripeness always verging
on rot. The yard-sale, take-me-please temptations of our hearts
like tawdry bullfight scenes or sweet Delilah's shears
on Samson's curls (her haremed by girls—in oil-painted corsets—

on the Louvre's dark walls). Is it any wonder Carry Nation came to call?
To cut the crushing velvet of desire down to size? *Your loving home crusader*
come to hatchet loose whiskey spilling gold like rococo frames. Pint glasses
held to hide the fear of hands; the rickety bar-stool spinning
of this life. *That bulldog running at the feet of Jesus,* baring her teeth. Save

us from us. The nails, the shattering light; the beautiful, weakening knees.

Matryoshka (as Madness)

If you could start
at the center: nest
a solid self inside
a safer self
like a house
so no one sees
all the ways you've
twisted open, copied
yourself. How you
don't knock down
the nesting wasps
from your back porch
eaves, the yard guarded
by copies of medieval
devils, their buzz
beautiful and maybe
deadly if a child knocks.
You are supposed to
make your home safe,
supposed to know dishes
from devil, but you still
throw plates for
their beautiful shatter
when it's all too solid
or isn't. Houses burn
quick as the air
between bodies.
It scares you to know this.
To know so little
of how to throw your self
into adulthood
like a voice.
The one solid wood
doll is the smallest:
trapped inside wood

inside air inside wood
like a prayer in a crucifix
you don't know how to
believe in, the church
only solid as
the ripped-roof blue
the congregation
stares into in Siqueiros,
their prayers like a windbreak:
pale trees in the sure belief
of storm. Above,
the devil hovers,
arms like a combine,
thrashing, threshing
their stares. It's best not
to look up when the sky
opens, sure of
nothing but opening.
Maybe all bodies
are storms, hurricanes
twisting up from
water, thrashing inside
them whatever else
you are. Your nephew
breaks down, breaks
open his house, is
wrestled into handcuffs,
locked up for safety.
A doll inside the body
of a glass-eyed doll.
Who would you ask for
if you called? Glass
shattered on your
floor, as if you're
trying to lock yourself

inside his mind.
Just south of him,
in Mexico, rising crime
means rising calls
for exorcisms. To unlock
the soul from the devil
like a knot pulled
from wood. The priests
say people summon evil
by praying to skulls.
Everyone praying
to their own hollows.

Suicide Notes (as M.C. Escher's Impossible Constructions)

Because finally I haven't   and the knife my mother raised
to chase me through the funhouse of our living room
screaming *Go ahead, if you're going to*   cut the ordinary
crescent suns of summer squash an hour later   with my hand
on its handle [suggesting self was impossibly contiguous]

If I believed in God I would be dead by now   No,
if I believed in a God like a knife drawer
I used to drive to churches in Springfield Missouri [the buckle
of the Bible Belt] and park outside because they were boxes
someone believed opened beyond the simple laws of ceilings

Someone told me [early] depression is a box and when I'm not
I see it as that cube I was so proud to learn to draw as a child
square overlaid on square and then those diagonals   [at first it seemed
like so much space] My mother said *Drawing boxes means you feel
trapped*   *Drawing flowers means you feel lonely*   [A doctor had electro-
shocked her in the 1960s   for *feeling too strongly*]

Maybe I am alive because despair
is so unoriginal   I did not question her   I was scared
I kept climbing stairs   [the winter in San Francisco I lived
leaning over bridges]   My almost-ex husband and my lover
had rolled the suicide   netting aside to make more space
for a rave in the air   I wore feather boas
I imagined as nooses   stayed up all night and felt

each morning like a square against a square and that diagonal
of the BART station stairs   like a tautology

because my students are waiting in the portable temporary classroom
that has been there for decades   I am climbing to teach them
because they believe I am
climbing to teach them they are
waiting   One had just been diagnosed at nearly fifty

as on the spectrum   was so relieved he kept telling me
he finally understood the walls inside his mind   another
was missing a finger   an artist
who looked like Diego Rivera   who I flirted with
because I was the cliché of melodrama   *Drawing a spinal brace*
and nails means
I was really hurting and if I had died then my last words
would more likely have been

Paragraph organization needs work.
Connection to thesis? than a note saying *I can't*

I can't I tried and family history of   and my nephew
will not in the future survive
a room of a gun and himself   and will leave no note
except his body

I don't believe in a God who wears a belt
he takes off for the rapture or a you-trespassed whuppin
I am not a melodramatic person
is one of my favorite lines of poetry because it climbs
up and down the staircase of its own denial

I have always been so careful to buckle
the seatbelt   I have spent months of my life in a box
like a buckle on a belt attached to something

Love itself was a form of domination so she made impossible
constructions of desire   I read of a poet who lived and died
before Escher made the print that in my teenage room's
imagination had never been imagined

[It was decades old already]
[my nephew has been dead a year] [my mother has been dead
more years than I was old when she used to call
Rise and shine   like I was the sun
meaning   come down the stairs]

It is winter again   I am in love
with my husband and the snow and a squash
called *delicata*   that sounds like it can't survive
though it cuts into perfect cubes   on the board that has never been level
that rocks like a mind against its own limits
that I have to keep steadying

I am using what I will call a *gravity knife*
even though that means something like a switchblade and this
knife isn't   Something has to explain what holds me
to the earth   why I get to make this impossible soup

Ofelia Has Not Seen Even One of the Seven Wonders of the World, and People Keep Making New Lists

Now the *largest poll on record* gives her this:
Christ the Redeemer, the tower, the martyr, the untouchable
jetliner wings of his grace. Standing underneath,
could a girl even see his face (struck twice by lightning),

or would she still be left imagining how he blesses
the sky, its sins of diffusion and cumulus? Her eyes
pulled up and up, like a flag raising off-key

bugle dawns at summer camp. Grass stickering her ankles.
It mattered—for some reason—just to stand there. To feel

responsible for morning, which would happen
anyway, which is maybe all wonder is: the Taj Mahal's white
minarets holding up grief as perfect symmetry—

as every single person born will die—a chain
so much longer than the Great Wall. All that rammed earth and hope

and erosion. And the story, for centuries, you could see
it from the moon. As if most people. As if a strand
of human hair a mile away. It makes her wonder
if we just want something huge enough to outlast our not

knowing if it really outlasts us. Those pyramids—
Chichen Itza, Giza in a country of car bombs—so much
sand colored like stone like sun it must be like
standing behind your own eyelids on a bright day,

phosphenes of ancient wonder, not real light: something firing
in your mind. All the gods buried in catsuits
of lapis and gold, and the tourists lining up like bottles

at a carnival. Throw the ring of *I have been the size*
of greatness around the neck. The game isn't rigged,

just impossible. A single perfect toss will win a big plush squid,
a tiger dangling like a striped stalactite. Mammoth Cave.
The London sewers. Hoover Dam. A snow cone

melting like the polar ice (still the top
of *7 Wonders to Visit Before They're Gone*) on your hands. Christ
can't even save his own. One finger broken off

in a second storm. She wants to say: They don't make gods
like they used to. But that's probably not true either.

You don't get to travel back in time to wonder, but
she'd like to. Once, in ancient Rome, the aurora borealis
flared so bright, firemen rushed out and tried to extinguish the sky.

At 14, I Would Have Traded Adulthood for a Role in *CATS*

because it was 1988, and fur made of legwarmers
was a new kind of animal
that could only be named by singing;

that I could stretch over my own dumb skin until
I shimmered and clawed. My unitard: the holy unity
of mind, body, better body. The stagelights

yowling for my beauty as I belted out a tragic past
of alleys, moonlight, magic, all of it

made up. There was only the present: the definition
of enlightenment. Now and another now

each night. A meow transformed into transcendence.
Gold eyes against darkness, someone to feed me

from a bowl that said, *You were always this*
creature—the ugliest tufts
of insecurity stitched into a perfect suit of self.

Never the audience, with its strange sad
costumes; underage girls with t-shirts for beer

they imagined as sunlight; real
memories; Arkansas towns holding paper-mill stench
between pine trees; a boy in a field; spine-scraping grass

and cicadas loudly hatching from dirt, singing
that song without words.

Sketch: Charcoal and Body on Paper

The girls who posed for Beginning Drawing,
insecurity slipped off their shoulders
and draped over chairs, knew how to turn themselves

into specimens—naked and safe
as feathers or bones or the amphibrachs of antlers;
how to suggest, like that, wildness and bodies in excess

of the bodies we could see. Their faces
when I'd pass them later in the hall, out of place,
too intimate to look at. Afterthoughts of neck

and breasts and hips. What I feared of my skin—
its proportion, perspective; the way I was always
and never really posing. How I wanted that beauty

that knew how not to care: let people
stare. Let them mismeasure,
smudge pages with charcoal, erase me.

Duchamp's *Nude Descending* Speaks

I've been there all along—not here, but where
the light shifts like the stutter when a phonograph skips
just slightly, the voice overlapping with its later

self—like *l'esprit de l'escalier*: what we think of after
on the stairs, that perfect retort, that wit
never synched to the moment. I've been here

on the brink of the landing, something truer
to tell you. My dream of one face. I tried holding still
even slightly, but my legs kept overlapping with later:

I was flamenco and nun. Accordion. Fan-fold and war
from two years in the future, the bodies already shipped
back. Their faces on the staircase—here where

time pleats into new reasons. Our hands: broken guitar
strings; machinery unable to touch. I was a flip-
book of women. A zoetrope in a movie—each later

nested inside the last one like regret. Each self over-
correcting. What should I have said? There is no step
that is not also stepping; where I am not everywhere
you imagine me, where I imagine myself too late.

How to Become Stained Glass

Audrey Munson, "Queen of the Artists' Studios," 1910

When the artist says, *A woman's feet are the most*
important items in her general scheme of beauty,
do what he says. Pick up marbles with your toes
one thousand times, learn to hold—still, slippery

as the streaks of fish beneath the savior's boat—
any pose he asks. Every piece of you must glow.

Some days, he needs an angel. A rainstorm. Arch
your foot like sadness. Learn to walk undressed
through heaven's narrow gates. *For bodies, clothes do harm—*
and worse for souls. Be architecture. Be guileless

in pretending to be sky. If he says, *so few girls possess*
figures which are beautiful, separated into their details,

learn fragmentation. The minute articulation of eyes
watching themselves. Blue-grey. A wisp of black
for hair or iris. If he orders you to stand still as ice
water deluges your back, understand he does not ask

for flesh, but soul, to uplift the falls. *The artist requires*
a leg that tapers. The artist requires a woman to supply

grace and emotion to the female form. Let him solder
you back together. Naked and chaste, restrained
and unfettered. Concentrate until you smolder
gold and garnet from the tips of your finger-panes.

The girl buttoned inside her dress may ache
like scraps of copper solder. Trade her for glass
that breaks only when it's told to break.

Ofelia Looks for *Anger* at the Metropolitan Museum

When she learned *women can be anything*, she didn't know
they just meant allegory. *Evening*'s one bare breast
sloping like moonlight toward her ribs, or *Beauty*'s dress

slipping past her nipples, skin smooth as—sweet wine? the soft bloom
of columbine? (when it used to mean a flower)—Or *Purity*
absconded from personality, that rustling hive of body

just winged marble soul now. It's terrifying. Like the rapture
or a taxidermied cat. All glazy eyes and curves
hardened to hold meaning in. How not one will ever flinch

or drop her thorn of vice, or wear a sweatsuit
with *Sweetie* written on the ass to sleep alone. It's hard to argue
specifics with a concept, but she wants to say *Memory,*

set the fucking mirror down. Stop gazing all dreamy
at *how dreams and youth must fade.* You're like a Barry Manilow
song, each word headed for ruin, like that Dietrich movie

where she played a model but the censors censored
all her posing, left the statues. Cut blood and flesh
and woman. *Song of Songs.* She's not a prude, but sometimes,

you can keep your clothes on, like in this atrium
air-conditioned so the art won't spoil. At least
Cleopatra (with her handy asp) has attitude. A name

you could name something living. *Here, Cleo! Here, Kitten!*
Here, Nydia, Blind Flower Girl of Pompeii. Everyone loves
a good martyr. How *resigned sorrow had banished her smile,*

but not her sweetness. How she's nobly groping
through rubble, breasts exposed to mean whatever
a woman's body means after a volcano explodes

and it's raining hot, invisible ash.

Geodes

I've stopped at that roadside, the stand with the jackalope,
its giant concrete antler-ears splitting blue desert
sky into myth and middle and other myth and middle, and if we're not
somewhere in the space between tuning-fork prong and listening for garnets
glittering so hard they metamorphosize to sound
inside us like the hum La Monte Young heard burn between telephone poles
from the step-down transformer in the Idaho fields—if we're not
that eternal drone that doesn't fit into unlikely and unpolished bodies and
has to fit the way the antelope steps down from its one skin
into the voltage of self as other self;
if there's not mythology like clumps of amethysts
growing like flowers at the heart
of everything—god help me, how do we continue if the words
of anger on the phone call matter more than the line? And if it's madness
to believe *we as humans are good at some core level*
as I tell a friend, a black man, knowing the risk he takes just walking
in a body with the perfect, jagged teeth of (name your favorite
jewel) invisible inside him, then, yes, I might be living in the fugue-like
dissociation of a gem state
in which I keep believing that bright, gorgeous
gaping in each of us will be enough
to save us: we'll carry each other carefully as geodes
to the cash register humming its raga of 60 hertz and ask
to see inside each other's lives like crystal castles
I visited as a girl who got to see a queen's rings gleaming
like the green glass my mother wore as emeralds
for recitals as a piano teacher with rhinestone cat-eye glasses
and a beehive hairdo, as if she were trying to pick up signals far beyond
Chopin—the mad beautiful sounds of the universe scorching
the underworld inside her where she'd lost her father to war
and white blood cells of cancer would later form like pomegranate seeds
blanched of their ruby—my friend looking at me
as if I'd sprouted strange towers of ears—saying, *You really believe*
people are good despite everything? and my feeling myself glittering
dumb with the costume-jewelry glint of maybe only privilege

to think beneath the desert of this country—swastikas spraypainted
on cinderblock like history is cheap, repeatable graffiti; outlines of bodies
at the Black Lives die-in; bullets designed to *peel back like petals,*
to tumble inside the body, as if some bodies are circus rings,
as if compassion has finally evaporated like the Mediterranean Sea
entirely did during the Messinian Salinity Crisis—
there might be, again, whole caverns forming
unmelting icicles taller than electric poles: geometric forests
of pure glass arcing (if someone crawled inside) the most unearthly earthly light.

Letters to Phryne

1. From the Sip N' Dip Mermaid Bar,
   Great Falls, Montana

I'm trying to understand pity that might
just be lust. Those judges calling you *impious*
til you bared your breasts in court to prove
you were too beautiful to hurt. I'm thinking
it must be nice to be a mermaid, even
if you're not, like Daryl Hannah (who swam here,
everyone reports until it starts to sound
dubious). To be the first Aphrodite. Virtue
sure, yet amphibious. Like piano-bar music
played by someone very old who says
these are standards so everyone mumbles
because they ought to know. Girl meets boy. Boy
paints her rising from the sea. The painting
is lost. Their eyes not like water around you,
not towel or robe. *A crime of grace,*
a later model writes, wanting to pose
for your story. Look what you left us: *la*
la la la. We still fall in love with what hurts us. We still
want to swim naked and it's still not allowed.
Want rumor just once to fit inside the truth
like beauty inside the soft fat of a breast, a scale
inside a sequin.

2. From The Houston Street Bakery,
   Fort Worth, Texas

Who cares if it doesn't exist now? Those cases hold
cream-puff swans as sure as history
holds you. Whipped feathers floating inside glass.

Was it true Hypereides thought to undress you? He—ghost-writer
turned to bodice-ripper. He was said to be clever.
Oratory as the art of praying: for dresses to be breasts'

white rotundas. There's no such thing as too much
grace. I longed for those swans.
I was too young to see beauty meant thin: blades

streaking ice on the rink. Everything
on the other side of glass so much cooler
than I was. Like a courtesan walking into marble.

The inherent potential for slippage between the body
and its meaning is tacitly acknowledged in art:
meaning sculptures of beautiful nude

women in Athens' squares don't mean women
are seen as beautiful when nude. You spent
your own money to rebuild its walls. Your

undraped Aphrodite copied for the Vatican
which doesn't exist yet. What ironies. Priests
haven't yet begun to molest boys. Enjoy

while you can. That cream, like spume from which Apelles
made Poseidon's horses rise. The sea disintegrating.
You still the sweet scandal of your own walled city.

3. From a Post-September-11th Anti-War Protest,
   San Francisco, California

Was it a relief to you, too? Becoming allegory?
Your back on the sidewalk outside KRON-TV,
the casualty already drawn? All you had to do
was play dead. (But again, I confuse us.)
Blue chalk outline. Blue jeans letting the cold seep
through. The reporters' lenses closed as
eclipses; another day I stopped outside Amnesia
Bar to watch the sun die
through a pinhole. There are tricks for not
burning out your eyes. Like closing them.
The reporters rushing past like fog on its way
to oxidize every statue in the city. Drape them like
a body on a gurney. Blue skin around the nails
of my mother's hands. Blue mechanical pencils
on her windowsill. A month after the war
started. Tell me what *unrelated* means, oh measure
of all things. Woman named both *toad*
and *goddess*. On October 27th my mother
dictated the recipe for perfect tiramisu,
joked *don't bake it too long*. On October 29th
she was a bag of ashes. In one story, you fake fire
in your lover's studio to learn which statue
was his favorite. If the world were burning,
and I were in time to save one thing? I lay down
in the lines of that body as if I fit there.

4. From Carrara, Italy

They say the quarry workers used to brag
Here even the stones are anarchists—these walls
so hard they broke men into radicals.

For every difficult beauty,
a bomb. Did you believe in the Fates? In something
like balance? Those kneeling angels—

the most perfect marble—with bloody knees.
I like the idea that the stone decides something:
Michelangelo's last Pietá devouring

all bodies to air. Christ's missing arm, a casualty
of that blue-grey anger. Or Praxiteles' chisel not stopping
at modest robes, not stopping

til a woman stood lifesize as his equal
before him. It cuts both ways.
A man *left his stain on the statue's*

thigh, overtaken by desire for you, for
Aphrodite. How did it feel to be *the first great*
realistic nude, as if your nudity were more capable

of living outside itself than other people's?
They call it *contrapposto.* That static sense
of movement. Call it God

with his rapey swan wings. Call it art or
terrorism. The stone asking and asking for it.

5. From Coney Island

[It] sets all one's ideas of the eternal fitness of things at naught.
Ad for Roltair's New Illusion of Pharaoh's Daughter

Am I not just using you as muse
if I keep asking questions? If I ask you

to question me back? Like Aphrodite
exclaiming to Praxiteles, *But when did you see me nude?*

The body's reality confirmed
by a goddess. Was it better before

boardwalks and irony? I'm watching
five grown men with driftwood etch a giant penis

into soft wet sand. Mothers scuttling off
children: Look: popcorn! Look: hotdogs! Did you feel

like a midway? Those red balloons marked *eternal*
fitness of things? All that air to shoot popguns

at nothing. *A lifeless marble statue turns into a living girl.*

Bangles bright as commandments. She's perfect
because she just became real. Should we ask her

to go skinny-dipping with us? She can leave her plaster
shadow on the beach. Let's find a booth with interesting

magic. Let's ask the Virgin about the wedding ring.
In one story, a man slides it on the finger

of her statue. Safekeeping while swimming. But
the statue won't ever release it. Moral: you can

marry anything. Moral? If it looks like a woman,
it is. Remember getting kicked out of Gifted

for taking every *Do Not Touch* sign

from the tour home? The teachers refused
to hear logic. *But they clearly meant furniture, not pieces*

of paper. Do you feel like that still? A label,
a little party hat of self,

folded over what someone says matters?

6. From Mount Rushmore

They lack, of course, a woman's human
scale: your Aphrodite draped around
herself, or Rufina Cambaceres leaned outside her
tomb in Recoleta—marble hands reaching
for the door she couldn't open. (Her
doctors had mistaken fainting for death. The guide says
see: the thinness of the arms is symbolic.)
Here, a mountain as body. A hydra. A god
with four bone-colored mouths. Jefferson had to be blown up
and started over. It's not painful,
for granite. *Living rock,* the guidebook says. *America, alive*
in stone. It's just idiom. No one
is supposed to live here. Though don't we all
want *the stone friend*, the statue that turns out
to be human? Even if, in some lights, it's hard to quite see
the difference. *It's dynamite!* It's all just puns: the democracy
of words electing two close meanings. Who is it that's looking back
when we *come face to face with history?*

7. From the Crazy Horse Memorial

Did you try to interpret your dreams?
This book says, *Be aware of yourself trapped in a statue.*
Once I was—awake—in an abstract painting. Bright

yellow body. Unspecifically naked. Like sliced fruit
in Montana winter. Dark paneling. My new husband's brush
touching only the canvas of my skin. It hurt to wait for myself

to appear. Yellow like cut roses by the Texas roadside. Slip
'N Slides on the flat lawns of childhood, my suit bunched
beneath me. That sticking that pretended

to be sliding. Crazy Horse galloping through a hundred
plaster models of himself. (They just make it seem more
unfinished.) *Whether you stumble across statues, or become one yourself,*

dreams of statuary can be challenging. No mouth
in my whole yellow face. It didn't strike me as strange then.
My husband liked to explain representation versus

abstraction. Crazy Horse didn't believe in
having his image made. Now he's a stone bridge pointing
toward becoming a finger. He'll be larger than Rushmore.

He would have called his own head desecration.
How can I not believe all fact—
like a later artist says—*is an abstraction of something?*

8. From Mexico, New York,
1920s home of Audrey Munson, "The American Venus"

Before she went mad, they say she put an ad
in the paper: *Seeking any man as beautiful*
as myself. Found her seventh love (prophecied husband),

an aviator, who never fell from her sky.
But that makes her sound shallow, the model
for a model. All those years of standing
still. Of mistaking a contrail for love.

Those unpaid nights at Diogenes' side,
did you learn cynicism before he invented
the word? Or is it true—*first whore with a heart*
of gold—you'd willingly give to the right man

all the beauty he could hold? Like grapes' dark
Dionysian rain before still lifes. A body
always at the center. A woman rollerskating
(stories say) down these dirt roads, balanced

by a lawnmower. A model in her 30s, put
out to pasture. Of course fashion skinned her
and kept on unrolling. Had she gone mad, or did
she only love the giddy feel of gravel

jolting? The fields scrolling past,
bumpy and true as Banvard's Mississippi panoramas
flooding through dry towns. Don't we all want
the movie that hasn't been invented yet? To be the grape

consumed and uneaten. Light
radiating like halos from our dented wheels.

9. From the Hamburger Kunsthalle, Germany,
   in front of Jean-Léon Gérôme's *Phryne Before the Areopagus*

I can't blame you for covering your face
at your own bare trial. You are blindingly
naked. Your skin's glowing
even now is almost too much to see. The sway
of one leg—fainting
into perfect contrapposto. As the jurors stare,
stunned and lecherous; red-robed as hemoglobin:
one body, democratic
and thoroughly male. *Haughty and electrical.* You can see it. Or
you can't. Your arms sparing
you that—that crooked, hand-clasped gesture
of modesty that covers nothing
modest women cover. As Gérôme would have it,
not sallow, but alabaster radiant so we gawk
(I gawk), guilty—*a crime of grace?*—we do not
turn away. You do it for us.
Tricky men. Always turning back the mirror. Or tricky
selves. Revealing everything and then not
looking. Is *the unseen proved by the seen?*
Eve, fig-leafing only her own eyes
and letting the world take her, naked as a rib.
God, the judge, as the first myth
of panorama. *An unbroken view,* from the Greek *horama,*
which means nothing like *whore,* though how could I not think of you, dear
stranger, self, *hetaira.* Didn't you see it too?
How every view keeps breaking?

Late American Aubade

Man in a chicken suit, you're the only one today
not selling beauty: 5th Avenue star-struck with Christmas,
three-story diamonds and flocks of ballerinas pirouetting
clockworking gears as if the Industrial Revolution
were a life-sized music box of desires and we've just kept
on winding. If. And Wish Upon. And shopping bag. And you
with your wind-ruffled feathers and flyers, pleading
for our primitive hungers. That inelegant grease spot
and crunch to remind us. The mannequins don't
even have bones. I'll never have a purse nice enough
to hold a wallet worth the money to buy the purse
at Barney's. And what does it matter? There are drumsticks.
I'm a vegetarian. You are no masked creature worth hugging
for a picture. No Minnie. No marble nymph of Beauty
in pigeon net outside the library, *old yet ever new eternal voice*
and inward word. As if we hear it clear in the gizzard,
Beauty is God and love made real. You will be this beautiful
if. You are the rock in the crowd-raked garden of traffic,
just past the corner of jaguar-made-of-dazzle and flapper
reading Shakespeare bound in bardic sparkles. Your yellow,
a scant flag to claim us, ordinary strange as holy chickens
in a gilded cage in Spain. Their ancestors, heralds
of a miracle. A huge mechanical owl recites Madonna
in a window Baz Luhrmann has been designing since February.
It takes all year for a miracle with this many moving parts.
All of us in a rush to wait for the *catastrophe of personality*
to seem beautiful again. As if this is the best we can hope for:
seeming to ourselves—like panhandlers dressed as Buddhist
monks the real monks are protesting. Asked for her secret,
the model for Beauty said, *The dimples on my back*
have been more valuable to me than war bonds. Asked for proof,
one orange-robed woman said, *I can't tell you where, but I do*
have a temple. Beaked promise of later lunch, catastrophe
of unbeautiful feather, how can we eat the real you
that you are not? Which came first? The shell to hatch
desire, or desire? Which skin holds my glittering temple?

Spread Spectrum

Not only did . . . [Hedy Lamarr] flee a loveless marriage to a Nazi arms dealer . . . and become (probably) the first Hollywood star to simulate a female orgasm on screen—she also took time out to invent. . . . Lamarr and composer George Antheil were awarded a patent in 1942 for a "secret communication system". It was meant for radio-guided torpedoes, and the pair gave [it] to the US Navy. It languished in their files for decades before eventually becoming a constituent part of GPS, Wi-Fi and Bluetooth technology.
Laura Barnett, The Guardian

A woman swimming nude in Prague in 1933:

breasts, two notes against dark water: its player piano

roll encoding the commonest refrain of *beauty*—the body

rippling onto film not as Jewish in this *Kampfzeit*

(*the time of struggle,* Germany's new Chancellor now

is calling it), but as music (who cares if it's mechanical? Her eyes

at the moment of orgasm, later, in close-up playing

synchronized desires, like Antheil's pianos, plane propellers,

drums inside a Paris hall, that futurist indecency

gusting hats off, listeners into riot) that sound, more than *glamour*:

how any girl can be, she'll later say, if only she *stands still*

and looks stupid: like a single, stilled frequency, a torpedo glittering

hullward through deep water. Let the sound carry,

hop frequencies, and no enemy can change its direction. She saw,

years before her remade face, how glitter is followed

by waste—how to not be where she seemed to be when a man

tried to watch her (all the copies of her) swimming on a loop called *his*, or how to chase the horse on which she'd draped

her clothes to bathe, the plot in harmless struggle to be anything

but her bare ass through fields, forests. And why should it be more?

There is no war yet in the world of *Ecstasy* and no invention,

or else, someone offstage is starting to play war: punch paper

with the notes that make the body carnage, and she's inventing

brilliance on the shore—so many frequencies at once—*All percussive.*

Like machines. All efficiency. No LOVE. The song separating

like a woman from her clothes (the future in careful disarray

to justify the present): the 88 keys of the piano spread

in waves, the Reich rising like a symphony past human hands, *indecency*

no longer just a shudder across her face. Because anything can only go

so far and then much farther. The camera—when it reaches the flinch

and lip of her—panning closer, closer, closer, then away.

Audrey Munson Committed to the St. Lawrence State Asylum for the Insane, 1931

You're back from Hollywood,
you tell the tabloids—
on a dais in *Heedless Moths.*
a scarf on your head
like prophecy.

At the Cecil Hotel,
you've swallowed mercury:
the neighbors' barns keep
tambourines, the world rattling—
It's not your fault you're not
where you posed all one summer:

facing opposite directions
from rescue,

only a child of stone. *But*
in your mouth: that psychic spies
like a security camera.
A girl pushes elevator buttons,
(anyone can see), signaling
water. On a locked-up roof,

elsewhere:
You are trained in allegory
You are heedless

spilling

a spy now. Or that's what
you're hunting
You pose with a tambourine,
as if to climb from a plane,
As a child, a psychic told me

people keep jumping
to die because I wanted to be
burning. You are
so many windows and
Kentucky Marble,
yourself as Sacrifice,

a lover laid in your lap
except he's dead.

the dead sea fruits of

It's not her fault
waving her hands
at nothing in the hall.
her body in that tank.
It's not your fault

they watched me like the spies
You are hunting
Sacrifice. Which is Duty?
they say. Now drink this.
through all the open taps.

Germans. Naked

propellers circling
I shall be famous and beloved

from just-built windows—
dead. It's not your fault
hunting Germans with
not enough people at home.
like in the Firemen's Memorial
and the figure of Duty—

like the Pietá. He'd rescue you.
To take his place:

happiness shall turn to ashes
from your past:
they haven't been invented yet.

Guests complain for weeks: foul

accidents keep happening

I was supposed to shadow.
moths.
That girl is safe in the future
No one is

Gem State

Because snakes unfasten something just below
my skin like those fields in Iceland that look pastoral—

(thick-wooled sheep & rivers if the gentleman painter with his linseed & oils
were on fire beneath his cap; his subterranean heat
boiling down the handle of his brush until the sheep steam
between geysers & sink holes & the churning & gulping of mud pits)

(*It's unusually hot,* said Maria, at the guest house, in the red-black
tradition of her apron. *Usually that means that something is going to blow up.*
Have some homemade blueberry skyr.)

(as if the world has migrating
arthritis like my mother with Lyme disease & any joint
can become a rift; any picnic basket packed with an earthquake)
(a geothermal park in the center of town
where there used to be a playground)—

I am afraid to go
into Gem State Jewelry
in my Idaho hometown because the owner keeps
in a glass-fronted antique jewelry case shaped like a roll-top desk,

a rattlesnake that lives, draping, sleeping, coiling & slipping weightless,
counterweighted down the polished shelves,
amid the rubble of amethyst & claddagh rings & rattled
chunks of onyx, those hooded eyes
like geodes that have broken open by themselves

& polished themselves & need nothing
to remind us there is no tidy ouroboros of eternity: just ruck-up
& unravel (my mother's Lyme disease really leukemia
not diagnosed yet) (the back of the case unclasped
like a necklace Saturdays for one white mouse)

& that muscular reach; those jaws, a locket's brass
unhinging to swallow a single snapshot of each ancestor
we'll never know who lives inside us—

like a sinkhole
steaming inside-out heat whole towns can fall into,
children sliding back down the coil of their umbilical
until all we have left is a thin rope that says *Caution*

that can't hold

the air back; the time
I stepped inside: it was raining, I saw something, I forget—
but that mouse had just been dropped

& there was stalking & thrashing & that mouth
coming closer & tourmaline & cat eye agate (every name fear
makes me hunger for) shining like wedding rings
I'd slip over my finger if I were brave enough
to marry this world

Tabloid Elegy

> *The suicide of this attractive American girl adds another name to the list of many women of refinement, breeding and culture who have in recent years come to a shocking end through disregard of the fundamental law of morality. . . and an immoderate love of luxury and gayety.*
>
> The American Weekly, *1921*

In the page-count of death, you're a scant halfway:
your string of pearls swung, innocent as a jump rope,

to the fold. As if you were still a child at a game
of Double Dutch. Skip: sidewalk and sky. Skip: Paris

and bathtub gin. Skip: virtue. Stockings on the radiator, legs bare
as new neon tubes. How could you know the charming host

meant you when he said "dancing girls"? Said "entertainment."
His accent bristled softly like cloves piercing an orange:

a pomander hanging in a room you kept entering
a little dizzy. What's that he said about the seven veils?

You liked the new revolving doors. How it felt to spin
in a storm of your own making. Who cared if Van Kannel invented them

because he didn't like to hold the door for ladies? Skip:
being a lady. Skip: being there at all. Those pillows like satin

lamps. Iridescence burning into morning. You should have been able
to wash off anything in all those fountains. How could you know

the fundamental law of doors—the ones that keep opening
keep closing behind you? Right below your breasts,

more florid headlines—*Choir Girl Ruined*
By Hate. Italian Chef Sued for Serving Queer Prunes. Why

Mrs. Halley Peck Had to Kill Herself. Crashed Balloonist
Lives by Eating Pigeons. Skip: no humiliations.

The Meteorologist Receives More Letters Asking

Please name the hurricane after my cousin *Faith*—who is a force of blow-dried hair and sorrow long as fake lashes. For *Gwen,* who crashes even parties she's invited to; folds sky instead of paper airplanes. *Judas.* (Too few people get named that.) *Me:* so we're all to blame for the damage. Hurricane *9-11; Civilian Collateral Damage,* Hurricane *Fill-in-the-Blank War. Ginger Rogers* or *Louis Armstrong*—like posthumous Oscars. All cosmic and spit-shined. *Ken Burns* for that fucking slide show. Let's pretend we'll linger on every body. Call this one *Baba Yaga.* Hurricane *Witch Baby. The-Earth-Gnashing-Its-Iron-Teeth-to-Eat-You.* Hurricane *Pre-school Teacher* gluing styrofoam fangs onto socks, like the world was the safe kind of floppy, we were all its creators. Hurricane *World Bank, Housing Crash, Hipster-hibiscus-donut-and-tea-shops-named-Bloom-and-Spoon-are-eclipsing-my-neighborhood.* (Don't name it *Spoon,* please). *Godiva.* I've always liked that. Naked as a high-pressure system. Give it a Christian name. A name that seems personal. George Carlin says, *No one cares about people killed by a number.* Hurricane *Voter Fraud.* Don't name it *Sandy Hook, Columbine*—places not the people who died there. Wait til after. - - - - - - - - - - - - - - - - - - Fill in the lives between hyphens. Hurricane *Hurricane* at *#Hurricane.* Please call it *Batman. Black Lives. Grace.* (I'm Catholic & when God makes me kneel at a child's funeral, it still feels like whiplash.) Hurricane *Scary-grin Emoticon. Loneliness-is-kudzu-with-a-head-start-on-everything.* Have you ever been in one, Mr. Weather? It feels nothing like *Floyd.* Hurricane *My sister dropping dirt on my nephew's coffin with the same leather gloves she wears to feed the donkey he named as a boy.* Hurricane *Suicide* twisting his mind into Molotov cocktails—crumpling drafts of every love, thought, don't-pull-the-trigger. Hurricane *Gabriel*: annunciation trumpet blown by Chihuly—spiral dead-ends and glass-notes. Hurricane *Chora* for the empty space Plato says form passes through into form. Like the eye of a storm, a woman's body. My sister holding carrots out for *Neige* to crunch and nuzzle. Hurricane *Because there is no choice but to imagine the unbearable to bear it.*

Audrey Munson Reimagines Her Life as Still Life

Flowers are much harder than faces.
Alex Katz

To not need this mouth,
these hands to arrange. To have been as ordinary, as strange
a sound as orange tucked in a tiger lily's
bright Victrola horn. To have unlaced myself from every corseted
kick of the Dancing Dolls
and not been china doll at all, but china plate: vines and hard grapes.
Domestic and wild as a picnic.
Dunegrass and panic grass like upended knives. To be an excuse for light
on the boardwalk, the shore—
and then Manhattan turned to mute geometry behind a table's cloth,
slight cotton billows harder to paint
and paint again than any mouth. To have been worth looking at
for every streak and crumple and petal-
fleck; not an expectation of eyebrows and neck, but asters' purple
frill and blunt-cut stems. No hope
that the water will save them. To never have been the girl dreaming
music-box trinkets, an admired
face. No bloomer-ruffled stalk down winter streets. To have no story
to rearrange my lips to tell.
No single star, but a quick bouquet that makes a foreground
of any windowsill,
sweeping all the lives outside into squares of background light.
What would have mattered?
Not happiness, not loneliness. Peonies. A saucer's expressionless white.

Baba Yaga Invites Fort Worth Girl Scout Troop #23 for a Campout

An overnight trip in the great outdoors brings you closer to nature—
and to your Girl Scout sisters. You might watch a sky full of stars,
cook a meal on a stick, or share silly stories around the campfire.
Junior Outdoors Badge: Camper

Dear girls: It's normal to feel afraid at first
in the woods. Trees can resemble strange old men
with too many damp arms,
and no light snaps on when it senses motion.
Most of your life, you'll find, is like that.
Which is sometimes fortunate, sometimes sex-standing-up-
in-the-dark-in-a-cell-of-an-island-fort with tourists
passing just outside, oblivious, bleary
from snorkeling. There won't be a badge for that.
There won't be a badge for a lot of things. If you want safety,
you might think again
about your Planet Set. That pretty pink tent
stitched to the moon
is military surplus, big enough for a family
of refugees. Some people never go home. Some
turn into sticks, tell silly stories: *Remember*
when we didn't have canvas for walls? Don't worry.
These are first-world woods. A few Texas pines,
a man-made lake. The campfire smells like a PG forest fire, turns the air
all jittery. Or maybe the air turns the fire, embers
like ladybugs swarming a collapsing log.
Didn't you earn *Science & Technology*? You know then
about the *topsy-turvy physics of roller coasters.*
That may or may not help you.
There's no badge for remembering facts
at useless times. No badge for the things you can do
with your hands when you're frightened.
Your postcards call *What a good time, what a good time*
ahead of yourself

like you're chasing yourself. It's easy to lose sight
of perspective. That's why you have music.
That's why you all sing
"Love of my life, I am crying, I am not dying, I am dancing
dancing along in the madness, there is no sadness,
only the song of the soul." Doesn't that sound nice?
Just look at the stars. Just listen to somebody's mother
strum guitar to mean *you, you, you* in chords everyone also
recognizes. There's no badge to prepare you
for the ways this is not preparation.
The woods are self-cleaning. Meaning even sound
dies. Meaning bugs, bones, pine needles
stitching earth to earth
like bridges stitch island to island in the Florida Keys.
Mosquitoes blur the air like you're riding fast-
drunk in a future car. Your friend is driving—steering
with his knees as he pours himself whiskey, tells
stories of playing saxophone on cruise ships. Look
at the stars,
you'll say, leaning your head back. They look like brass, like fire
glowing in the middle of the wilderness of sea. Girls,
you'll set every log so carefully this first time
someone teaches. Crisscrossing, tamping
down the last hot embers. You'll, most of you,
outlive your own decisions.

Selfie with *Pomona: The Goddess of Abundance*

Pulitzer Fountain, New York City

She has all the advantage. Two sculptors
for her single body. Bronze prepossession. Bare arms
muscled as if she plucked each apple in her basket,
then scythed the reeds to weave the basket—heaping on peaches
and pearls of snow. What seasons?
What death? She's seamless as light. She doesn't even need
the fountain she's standing on—its layercaked Christmas trees
or summer spritzing. She's a one-woman waterfall
of whatever. Could toss the basket on my head—see
how she leans—then fill another. She could mint money
out of bird shit. Go everywhere in mink coats
and the minks still living. What climate change? What protests?
She doesn't even need breath in her body. She's her own
Roman Empire. The champagne porch of the Plaza
glassed-in now behind her. Bellinis for all
who can afford them. She's her own 1%
chance of radiance. The drizzle we try to catch
like that girl I watched turn all of Trinity Cathedral into self
with stained glass. Self with organ, self with hymnal, with column—
like she was a caryatid lost from her ceiling. I wanted to ask her:
isn't anything sacred? Why not find a belltower and think of God
and deformity. But how is that different? Self
with ancient story. Space shaped like what we're not
can conquer all desire. Self on a memory card can conquer
all questions. What price these smiles? These abundant
deletions? Where's the best light to look human?

NOTES ON THE POEMS

"Self Portrait as *Curious Lunatic's Sketch of a Dancing Girl*" references Anne Carson's *The Glass Essay*: "Soul is the place, /stretched like a surface of millstone grit between body and mind, /where such necessity grinds itself out."

"Ode to Theda": Theda Bara (Theodosia Burr Goodman) was a popular silent film sex symbol and "Vamp." Her name, an anagram of "Arab Death," was constructed by the film industry, along with a story about her being born in the Sahara. "Scandals of Classic Hollywood: The Most Wicked Face of Theda Bara" is by Anne Helen Petersen.

"The Altogether": Audrey Munson—known as "The Exposition Girl" (for modeling for more than a dozen statues for the 1915 Panama-Pacific Exposition) and as "The American Venus" and "The Queen of the Artists' Studios"—was early 20th-century America's most famous artists' model. Munson's face and body continue to be visible in allegorical statues, particularly in New York City, but Munson herself was, even during her lifetime, largely forgotten. Following mental breakdowns in her 30s, she lived, institutionalized, for more than another 60 years. Munson modeled for, among many statues, the statue of Memory in the Metropolitan Museum, Beauty outside the Schwarzman Building of the Public Library, and Pomona at the Pulitzer Fountain. Quotations in the Audrey Munson poems are taken, among other sources, from *American Venus: The Extraordinary Life of Audrey Munson, Model and Muse* by Diane Rozas and Anita Bourne Gottehrer, *Queen of the Artists' Studios: The Story of Audrey Munson* by Andrea Geyer, and from Munson's own 1921 columns "The Queen of the Artists' Studios" in *The American Weekly*. To pose "in the altogether" is to pose nude.

"Suicide Notes (as M.C. Escher's Impossible Constructions)" is dedicated with deep gratitude to Alisa. "I am not a melodramatic person" is from Anne Carson's *The Glass Essay*. "Love itself was a form of domination . . ." is a combination of Margaret Homans' claim about Emily Dickinson and Shawn Alfrey's response to it in Alfrey's *The Sublime of Intense Sociability: Emily Dickinson, H.D., and Gertrude Stein.*

"Ofelia Looks for *Anger* at the Metropolitan Museum" loosely quotes from *The Last Days of Pompeii* by Edward George Bulwer-Lytton.

"Letters to Phryne" are addressed to the 4th-century-BC courtesan and artists' model known as Phryne, who posed for the first famous statue of Aphrodite. (Audrey Munson, in turn, is quoted as saying she wanted to pose as Phryne.) Phryne was famously tried for indecency for swimming naked and then acquitted after her lawyer had her bare her breasts to the jurors, a scene rendered in Jean-Léon Gérôme's *Phryne Before the Areopagus*. Quotations used in the series include *The Dream Directory* by David C. Lohff, *Queen of the Artists' Studios: The Story of Audrey Munson* by Andrea Geyer, and Walt Whitman. "All fact is an abstraction of something" is William Kentridge.

"Late American Aubade" quotes Imelda Marcos, Audrey Munson, and Frank O'Hara.

"Spread Spectrum" quotes, among other sources, George Antheil's own description of his *Ballet mecanique*: "all percussive . . ."

"Audrey Munson Reimagines Her Life as Still Life" was inspired by a tribute to the artist Jane Freilicher that I attended in New York City in 2014; Alex Katz was praising Freilicher's work when he said, "flowers are harder than faces."

"Selfie with *Pomona*" references Allen Ginsberg's "A Supermarket in California," and also Frank O'Hara's lines "Oh space! / you never conquer desire, do you?"

ACKNOWLEDGMENTS

Deep thanks to the editors of the following journals for first believing in and publishing these poems, sometimes in earlier versions:

Alaska Quarterly Review: "Ofelia Plays Like a Girl"; *American Literary Review*: "Baba Yaga Appears in Feminist Theory Class and Gives an Impromptu Lecture" and "Ode to Theda"; *Barrow Street*: "How to Become Stained Glass"; *Beloit Poetry Journal*: "In the Case of Mme. Zina Brozia, of the Paris Grand Opera Versus M. Jean Metzinger, Cubist"; *Blackbird*: "Audrey Munson Reimagines Her Life as Still Life" and "Baba Yaga Invites Fort Worth Girl Scout Troop #23 for a Campout"; *Breakwater*: "At 14, I Would Have Traded Adulthood for a Role in CATS" and "End Times"; *Cascadia Review*: "Driving After Rain," "The Louvre Saloon, San Jose: Hatchetation (1903)," "Requiem for No Hands" and "Sketch: Charcoal and Body on Paper"; *Cimarron Review*: "Late American Aubade"; *Copper Nickel*: "Matryoshka (as Madness)" and "Tabloid Elegy"; *Cream City Review*: "Duchamp's *Nude Descending* Speaks"; *Mid-American Review*: "The Altogether"; *Pleiades*: "Selfie with *Pomona, The Goddess of Abundance*"; *Poetry Northwest:* "The Hungry Eye"; *Santa Clara Review*: "Audrey Munson Committed to the St. Lawrence Asylum for the Insane, 1931" and "Baba Yaga Rides It's A Small World"; *Southern Humanities Review*: "Spread Spectrum"; *The Feminist Wire*: "Ofelia Looks for *Anger* at the Metropolitan Museum"; *The Missouri Review,* "Letters to Phryne" and "Ofelia Has Not Seen Even One of the Seven Wonders of the World, and People Keep Making New Lists"; *Willow Springs*, "Self Portrait as Curious Lunatic's Sketch of a Dancing Girl" and "The Giant Artichoke". "Matryoshka (as Madness)" was also featured on Verse Daily.

Eternal gratitude to *The Missouri Review* for selecting "Letters to Phryne" and "Ofelia Has Not Seen Even One of the Seven Wonders of the World, and People Keep Making New Lists" for their 2014 Editors' Prize, and to the University of Idaho for a 2014 Kurt Olsson Early Career Fellowship to research Audrey Munson in New York City—both foundational to launching this project. And to those who have written and made art about Audrey Munson, particularly Andrea Geyer for her project *Queen of the Artists' Studios*. For creative conversations and inspiration, I'm so grateful to Stacy Isenbarger, and our two BASK interdisciplinary arts collaborators, Belle Baggs and Kristin Elgersma, as well as my amazing University of Idaho students (including four inspiring Women and Poetry classes) and colleagues, including Robert Wrigley and Michael McGriff. Thank you, David Thacker and Elizabeth Bradfield, for your comments; to the Port Townsend Writers' Conference community for the last push; to Emily Van Kley for your eleventh-hour insights; and, always, to Gabriel Fried and Persea for your caring support of my work. Dylan Champagne, none of this would be without your love, your insight on my poems, and our life together. And finally, deep love to my sister Anne, my nephew Nathan, and the memory of my nephew Gabriel, who loved poetry, particularly John Ashbery's "The Ecclesiast."